# 12 Wheels
## of KARMA

# 12 Wheels *of* KARMA

*Astrology as a tool for
meditation and self-inquiry*

HUNTER REYNOLDS

flaming seed
press

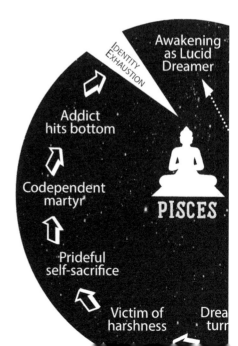

IDENTITY EXHAUSTION

Awakening
as Lucid
Dreamer

Addict
hits bottom

Codependent
martyr

PISCES

Prideful
self-sacrifice

Victim of
harshness

Drea
turn

ISBN 978-0-9892605-0-3

Book design: Jane Brunette

Cover photo: Vitezslav Valka
Part 1 photo: Joe Pena
Part 2 photo: Piotr Clutcha
Part 3 photo: Lauren Graham

Published by Flamingseed Press
flamingseedpress.com

# Table of Contents

# PART ONE
# The Spin We're IN

# Astrological archetypes are not primarily ways of understanding personality; they are spinning, karmic wheels designed to be meditated upon while resting at their hub.

THE MORE WE TUNE IN to our own or another's spinning archetypal circumference, the more heartless it feels not to provide a compassionate, witnessing center. From here, we see what personalities really are: meditative prods.

Think about that. This means that every ego we encounter is a banging, badly-loaded dryer on spin cycle, searching our eyes for a firm ground of Being. No matter how seamless their shtick, the believed-in personality is a lonely cry for love, and our reflexive like or dislike of them is equally disappointing to their souls.

What's that you say? You didn't sign up to be the vast, empty center of every hairdo'd spin cycle that crosses your path? I mean, that's a lot of human stories to provide hubs for, no? Not so fast. What if, instead of encountering an endless parade of personalities, we see only the archetype-inlaid belt of the Divine Being wheeling around us like dots of light in the night sky? In this scenario, there is only one personality to work with and the stars on the belt are as manageable as we are mystical.

$S$TILL, it appears that we have karma with certain archetypes. This demands that we draw their human representatives closer to us. It doesn't matter if they are a friend, a foe or someone we claim to feel indifferent towards; from the second we meet them, these folks become orphaned creatures prowling our subconscious, begging us to remember, for them, who they truly are. And why should we be their John the Baptist? Because

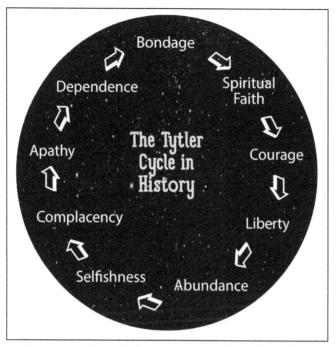

The Tytler
Cycle in
History

Bondage
Spiritual Faith
Dependence
Courage
Apathy
Liberty
Complacency
Abundance
Selfishness

**This cycle of world history is commonly attributed to 17th century Scottish historian Alexander Tytler.**

they are unforgiven aspects of our past or present ego; failing to "remember for them" makes the belt disappear and the faces bob pointlessly in space.

Why did we climb back onto this wheeling rock? Perhaps to admit that our uninvestigated, interpersonal likes and dislikes are ego's way of thumbing its nose at the mirrors existence provides so that we might practice staring straight and steady into the eyes of the Beloved. Who are we, truly? A connoisseur of wheels.

CONSIDER the wheel of history, attributed to 17th century Scottish historian, Alexander Tytler. Is not this incremental creep from grace to complacency to bondage and back again to grace the essential activity of the unwitnessed mind — the larger wheel within which our daily thoughts and feelings spin? How could a government or individual ego possibly avoid being dragged around this kind of wheel, except by following some kind of spoke-like dharma back to its undizzied center?

Astrology, it turns out, is the study of just this kind of wheel where the spinning vault of the constellations above us serve as a steady reminder of the corresponding archetypal wheels spinning within. The inward-leaning spokes of the wheel? Meditation and archetypal self-inquiry.

SOUNDS GOOD, you may say, but how exactly does one use the astrological archetypes to move to the meditative heart of this wheel? Begin by browsing through the 12 wheels that follow in part two. Then when you're ready to dive in, go to part three and choose the self-inquiry meditation that best suits your current circumstance.

# The question at the heart of every wheel: Will we return

to the timeless, witnessing presence

that we are with minimal stress

by breaking the momentum

of the wheel at the window of sanity,

or will we crawl back into Timeless Being

via sheer identity exhaustion?

# PART TWO
# 12 Wheels of KARMA

# Wheel of
# **Individuation**

*Pioneering presence to dispirited dupe*

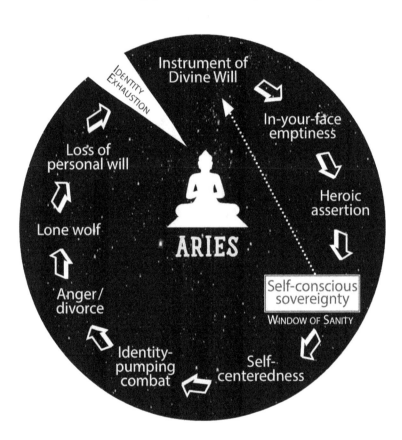

Instrument of Divine Will

IDENTITY EXHAUSTION

In-your-face emptiness

Loss of personal will

Heroic assertion

Lone wolf

**ARIES**

Self-conscious sovereignty

WINDOW OF SANITY

Anger / divorce

Identity-pumping combat

Self-centeredness

## WINDOW OF SANITY: SELF-CONSCIOUS SOVEREIGNTY

*S*overeignty is an illusion on loan from the Divine. It was given to us so we might learn how to walk the somebody/nobody tightrope — to be mad enough to be mortal, sane enough to disappear. The result? A healthy interpersonal synapse across which to send the Divine spark. Standing at the center of the Aries wheel gives us the ability to generate Divine heat and experience full-spectrum intimacy.

In this brief window of sanity, we still have a choice: Will we continue descending into the myopic thrill of personal will, or circle back for a swig of the storyless presence that interpenetrates and connects us all? Will we remember that sovereignty is an illusion on loan from the Divine and allow this humbling realization to infiltrate our day-to-day actions, or claim ownership of will and allow our divinely endowed courage to devolve into antagonistic friction and spirit-severing defeat?

# Wheel of
# **Embodiment**

*Sensual christening to toxic flush*

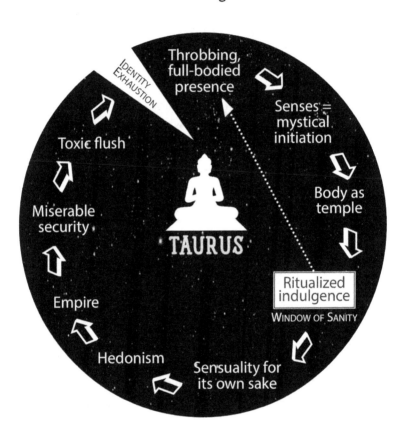

- Throbbing, full-bodied presence
- IDENTITY EXHAUSTION
- Senses = mystical initiation
- Toxic flush
- Body as temple
- Miserable security
- Ritualized indulgence
- WINDOW OF SANITY
- Empire
- Hedonism
- Sensuality for its own sake

TAURUS

Our senses do not belong to us; they are delirious, meditative doorways designed to dissolve the story of the separate self so we might go skin-to-skin with the One Being. What happens when we use more and more of our pleasuring to catapult us into union with Spirit? In short, ego death. The senses satisfy beyond our mind's ability to enjoy them. In each episode of spirit-glorifying sensuality, we practice lifting the burden of the separate self before death can pry it from our elderly hands.

At this juncture, while a hint of ritual still surrounds our sensual indulgence, we can still remember what prayerless consumption is: a squandered opportunity to lavishly embody the Great Unknown. Will we return to the fullness of Being for some ego-dissolving body prayer, or succumb to the undertow of ego-hardening sensuality?

# Wheel of
# Inquiry
## *Innocence to ennui*

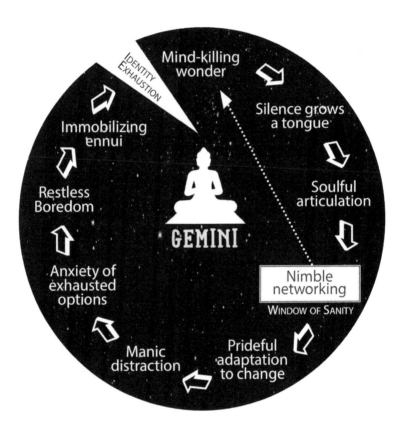

Identity Exhaustion

Mind-killing wonder

Silence grows a tongue

Immobilizing ennui

Soulful articulation

Restless Boredom

GEMINI

Nimble networking

WINDOW OF SANITY

Anxiety of exhausted options

Manic distraction

Prideful adaptation to change

There are thoughts that take us to the cliff edge of thought. Buddhism calls this breed of synaptic firing "dharma." Life constantly veers us toward this kind of void-friendly thought and speech. It takes years (and lifetimes) of karmic conditioning and willful compliance to bonsai our innocent, self-inquiring wonder into indiscriminate data-gobbling and ego-enhancing gab.

In the throes of nimble networking, while speech and thought are still in service to interpersonal bonding — if not soulful union — a moment comes when we have a choice: Will we continue descending into a prideful, pivoting identity that uses the rush of experience to distract itself from the "condition of all conditions," or return to the center of this wheel to rededicate our attention, speech and thought to the ego-dissolving mystery directly in front of us?

# Wheel of
# Nurturing
*Mothering to melancholy*

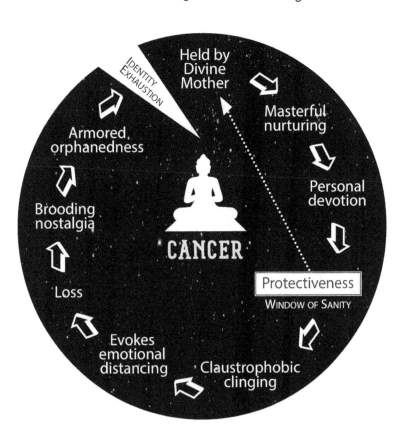

Held by Divine Mother

Identity Exhaustion

Masterful nurturing

Armored orphanedness

Personal devotion

Brooding nostalgia

CANCER

Loss

Protectiveness

WINDOW OF SANITY

Evokes emotional distancing

Claustrophobic clinging

## WINDOW OF SANITY:
## PROTECTIVENESS

There are little ones within us that never completely grow up, and these we sign up to understand and care for when we enter into any messy, mortal relationship. Over time, these little ones start making demands. What began as a spontaneous gush of care turns into a business deal: "I give you love; you receive it in a way that my insecurities and wounds from the past stay unconscious and unfelt." Suddenly, it is our loved one's job to protect us from ourselves. At this point, our partner has few options: collude with our myopic version of caring, challenge us to spiritually "grow up," or realize our worst dreams by pulling away.

In this brief window of sanity, we still have the opportunity to follow the spoke of good-hearted protectiveness back to the hub of Divine Mother love. Will we gently rock ourselves from our maternal center, confessing the insecure, self-referencing quality of our love, or engage in a manipulative nurture that sows dependency and obligation, inching us toward the orphanedness we fear?

# Wheel of
# Self-worth

*Radiance to defamation*

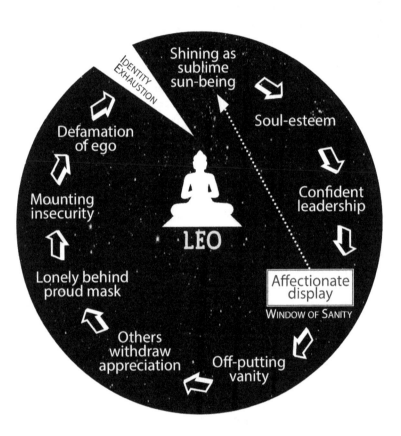

Shining as sublime sun-being

IDENTITY EXHAUSTION

Defamation of ego

Soul-esteem

Mounting insecurity

Confident leadership

Lonely behind proud mask

Affectionate display

WINDOW OF SANITY

Others withdraw appreciation

Off-putting vanity

LEO

## WINDOW OF SANITY: AFFECTIONATE DISPLAY

R adiant affection is like the sun: it turns people into revolving planets. Affectionate display, on the other hand, points to an insecure ego fishing for a good review — if only from themselves. As such, it is a still-manageable form of divine pride that can be caught before it drifts into off-putting vanity. Only when we catch our ego dancing before the mirror of another do we have the chance to get off this degenerating cycle of self-worth.

Will we use this brief window of sanity to confront the mounting insecurity of our ego masquerading as magnanimity, or cross over into off-putting vanity? Will we prayerfully purchase a first-class ticket back to the spontaneous radiance at the heart of everyone, or continue drifting into flamboyant pride with its attendant stink of soul-defamation?

# Wheel of
# Service

*Tao to disgrace*

Slave to the Tao

Karma Yoga

Devotion to healthy systems

Exacting Efficiency

WINDOW OF SANITY

Clinical distancing

Heartless critique

Isolating Perfectionism

Struggle against entropy

Disorienting loss of ideals

IDENTITY EXHAUSTION

VIRGO

Efficiency gets dangerous when it becomes exacting. Why? Because it's the first sign that ego is trying to squeeze the fruits of spiritual practice from the mechanics of physical matter. Over-ordering and critique are our first whiffs of the drift toward spiritual materialism.

In this window of sanity, we have the chance to catch when our longing for meditatively earned glimpses of the soul's purity begin to be substituted with hopes for immaculate health and serviceful perfection. Alas, if the ego were honest, it would admit that it depends on the eroding, phenomenal world to provide edges for its proud and lonely me-story. How does spirit see the world? As a whirling, psychotropic stage set, unimprovable in its ability to catalyze compassion. If at the first signs of tightness and perfectionism we return quickly to the center of this wheel for a glimpse of the Divine guiding us step-by-step through samsara, we have spared not only ourselves, but all those around us a boat-load of anal stress.

# Wheel of
# Relationship

*Harmony to estrangement*

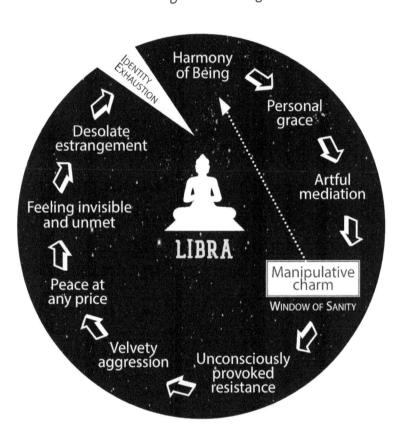

Harmony
of Being

IDENTITY
EXHAUSTION

Personal
grace

Desolate
estrangement

Artful
mediation

Feeling invisible
and unmet

LIBRA

Manipulative
charm

WINDOW OF SANITY

Peace at
any price

Velvety
aggression

Unconsciously
provoked
resistance

## WINDOW OF SANITY:
## MANIPULATIVE CHARM

The line between spontaneous, heartfelt harmony and agenda-ridden charm is thin, but not imperceptible. The sooner we catch our unconditional positive regard for the mystery of another's soul devolving into intimacy-killing politeness, the less likely it is that the subtle violence and objectification in our charm will build up, at a later date, into rawness-restoring conflict.

In this window of sanity, while our heart is still genuinely—if imperfectly—engaged, we have the opportunity to inwardly pause and confess the soul-dismissive self-centeredness in our posturing. Instead of trying to live up to an image of ourself as "caring," we can now innocently open and feel into what life wants in this encounter. We can circle back to our inner being and allow the unforced sense of connection to decide the form and direction of the relating.

# Wheel of
# Transmutation

*Kali to criminal*

Awakening to the Deathless

IDENTITY EXHAUSTION

Self-stinging repentance

Shamanic facilitation

Isolating aura of intimidation

The Detective

SCORPIO

Seizing psychic control

Fascination with innocence in depravity

WINDOW OF SANITY

Entering the underworld

Taste for the forbidden

I t is a sign of nondual wisdom when we can see the innocence in the twisted and perverse. This allows us to engage with the dark dance of our own and other's ego death and painful self-reckoning without losing faith in the light at the end of this passage. The problem comes when we start forming a prideful, shadow-hound identity that requires increasing doses of darkness to pump up its sense of potency. At some point, we start over-estimating our ability to transmute the inner and outer grit into grace, and our healthy carnal curiosity turns into impotent obsession.

In this brief window of sanity, while tenderness and consideration still motivate a good portion of our attraction to the forbidden, we still have the wherewithal to let the shadow-hound ego die back into the unconfessed beauty of mundane, everyday life. From here, we can let the soul's forbidden innocence take us apart. Our half-hearted detective ego then rests in the mind-killing Divinity everywhere.

# Wheel of
# Mentorship

*Oracle to nihilist*

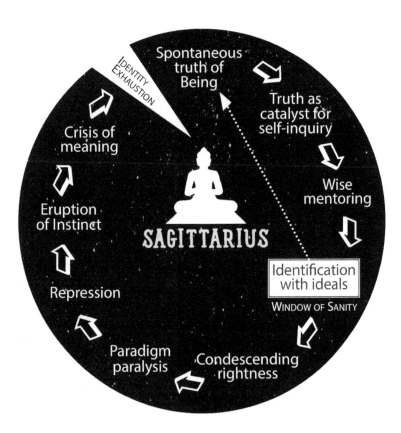

Spontaneous truth of Being

IDENTITY EXHAUSTION

Truth as catalyst for self-inquiry

Crisis of meaning

Wise mentoring

Eruption of Instinct

SAGITTARIUS

Repression

Identification with ideals

WINDOW OF SANITY

Paradigm paralysis

Condescending rightness

Having a defensible opinion is a sign of intellectual maturity in most circles. The problem comes when we start believing that beliefs and opinions say something about who we actually are and that our synaptic snapshots have no element of theory in them. In this window of sanity, while there is still some openness and inquiry in our philosophizing, we have the chance to circle back for a humbling shot of the ineffable truth of Being.

By doing this, our paradigm stays supple and we spare both ourselves and our "students" the pain of shattered ideals and cynicism down the road. The Ineffable seems to like inspiring others with passionate, provisional perspectives, but now is the time to ask ourselves, "Are my big-picture truths inspiring my own and other's continuing self-inquiry, or are they cluttering up the eyes of direct seeing?"

Sagittarius

# Wheel of
# Authority

*Mission to ambition*

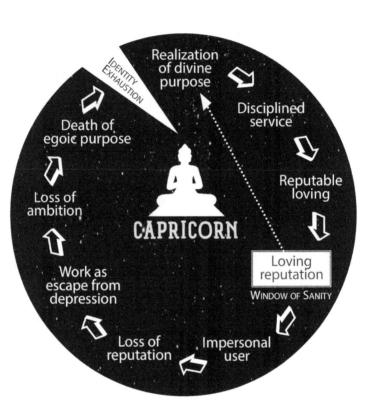

## WINDOW OF SANITY:
## LOVING REPUTATION

Working to improve one's reputation for the sake of opportunities to influence and care for others is not unhealthy. It is, however, flirting with the possibility that we will become identified with reputation and role at the expense of vulnerable presence. In this window of sanity we have the chance to assess whether social status is becoming more important than the risk of authentic, personal caring.

Should we persist on this ambition-over-empathy path, business-speak will gradually infiltrate and harden our heart-speak, and more and more people will feel creeped out by our strategic way of relating. Will we now circle back to feel into our soul's incarnational calling? Or will our pursuit of horizontal success inch us toward interpersonal aridity and a role-bound life?

# Wheel of
# Community

*Visionary to drop out*

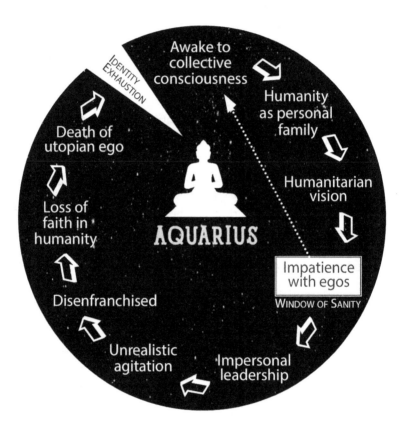

Awake to
collective
consciousness

IDENTITY
EXHAUSTION

Death of
utopian ego

Humanity
as personal
family

Humanitarian
vision

Loss of
faith in
humanity

AQUARIUS

Impatience
with egos

WINDOW OF SANITY

Disenfranchised

Unrealistic
agitation

Impersonal
leadership

## WINDOW OF SANITY:
## IMPATIENCE WITH EGOS

Few people feel guilty judging face-less corporations. In this window of sanity, utopian fixation has not yet blinded us to the plight of individual egos. Here, we can still remember what entrenched, self-serving organizations really are: a collection of orphaned egos whose spiritual need for a sense of oneness, or shared identity, has devolved into a merely human sense of belonging. This misplaced but well-intentioned devotion to a materialist sangha has blinded them to the wake of their miniature society.

Will our earth-loving idealism harden our hearts to those individual souls struggling, over lifetimes, to overcome their numbness to the group mind? Or will our activist path become a serendipitous, moment-to-moment encounter with the collective consciousness shining from every pair of eyes — even as we educate and agitate for change?

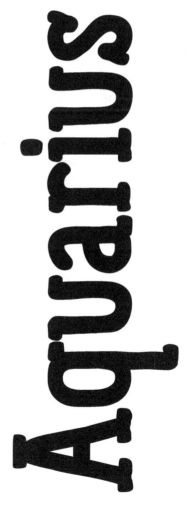

# Wheel of
# Compassion

*Mystic to martyr*

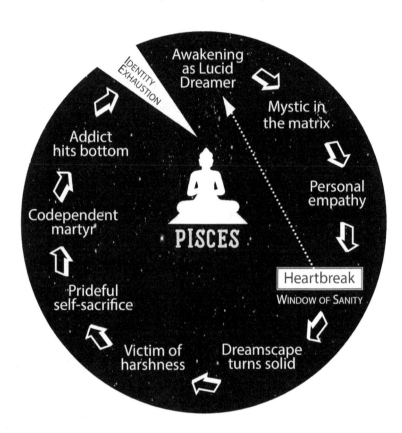

Awakening as Lucid Dreamer

IDENTITY EXHAUSTION

Mystic in the matrix

Addict hits bottom

Personal empathy

Codependent martyr

PISCES

Prideful self-sacrifice

Heartbreak

WINDOW OF SANITY

Victim of harshness

Dreamscape turns solid

## HEARTBREAK

Few are spiritually gutsy enough to feel into the collective suffering of a planet full of eternal souls dreaming they are dying bags of flesh. The hearts of those who do will, of course, break. At this point on the wheel, while the dreamlike illusion of separation is still heartbreakingly palpable, we have a choice: invest deeper into contact with the undivided Presence (via meditation and self-inquiry) or allow the dream to turn more and more solid, pushing us to exhaust and martyr ourselves in a desperate attempt to redeem and forgive it.

In this window of sanity, heartbreak becomes a cue for us to vision quest our way back to the center of this wheel for some sweet sips from the spring of meditation. To fail this call for mystical refreshment is to join forces with the nightmare and turn all of our generous gestures of love into secret feedings of the paradigm that victimizes the souls we claim to be helping.

# PART THREE
# How to Use the WHEELS

**R**emembering that each of the twelve astrological wheels of karma is only one of many possible versions of how the archetypes spin within and around us, I invite you to humbly inquire into how these slippery cycles of forgetting and remembering impact your life, relationships and habits of mind. The more shrewdly we witness these wheels in action, the more motivated we are to stand strong at their hub.

There are three ways to work with these wheels:

*As a proactive daily spiritual practice.*

*As a means of identifying and working with your own cycles of suffering.*

*As a way of cultivating insight and compassion for another ego.*

In the end, there is little difference between these last two approaches. Whether a wheel spins within or without, it's showing up in our space. This makes it our wheel to heal — our karmic challenge to stand strong at its hub. Is there another option? Oh yes: live a lonely, unguided life riddled with pointless interpersonal accidents.

One more thing: don't just hone in on your sun, moon or ascendant. Other factors in your birth chart and current transits may be asking you to concentrate on an entirely different wheel. Let go of your astrological preconceptions and feel into the flow of each wheel until it chooses you.

# USING THE WHEELS as a proactive, daily spiritual practice

### 1. Set your intention
Begin by thinking of those you come into contact with every day, and the impact you have on them when you receive them with compassion versus when you receive them with reactivity. Set an intention to enter this practice deeply not just for yourself, but for them.

### 2. Circle
Circle around the first wheel and take note of the point that best describes your present state of consciousness. When you are finished, circle around the wheel again — this time pausing at the wheel of sanity to read the corresponding text. Then close your eyes and ask yourself: "What would I have to let go of in order to embody a more awakened phase of this wheel?" Instead of grasping for a rational answer, allow the spirit of this question to create an atmosphere of heartfelt petitioning. If an answer or

image comes, give thanks and move on to the next wheel. If not, trust that the sincerity of your asking will bear fruit later.

### 3. Dedication: Forgive the dream
When you are finished with all twelve wheels, dedicate your practice to the countless number of souls who are, even now, being ravaged by these wheels:

> *Now that I see how gradations of lying*
> *are the best our staggering, wheel-dizzy psyches can muster,*
> *I understand the pain that these lies*
> *cause myself and others*
> *is as evil as sunrise, as sinister as sunset.*

Finish by sitting quietly, praying that the fruits of your practice might inspire all beings to be released.

## USING THE WHEELS to inquire into active, personal suffering

### 1. Set your intention
Begin by thinking of those you come into contact with every day, and the impact you have on them when you receive them with compassion versus when you receive them with reactivity. Set an intention to enter this practice deeply not just for yourself, but for them.

### 2. Circle
Begin by circling once around each of the twelve wheels without reading their corresponding window of sanity. Make a list of the wheels that, upon first reading, evoke the most feeling in you.

### 3. Contemplate
Choose the wheel that best captures the theme or themes you are currently challenged by. Read the text for this wheel's window of sanity, then feel your way around and around this wheel, each time pausing at the window of sanity to feel, contemplate and visualize what new attitude or action you might take in order to break free from this cycle and rest at its lucid center.

### 4. Be released
Continue feeling your way around this wheel until you feel yourself being released from its grip. (This may take numerous sittings.)

### 5. Return to your first impression list
When your work with this wheel feels complete, return to your first impression list and ask yourself, *Which wheel is crying out loudest for a witness now?* Repeat the practice with that wheel.

### 6. Dedication: Forgive the dream
When you are finished, dedicate your practice to the countless number of souls who are, even now, being ravaged by these wheels:

*Now that I see how gradations of lying
are the best our staggering, wheel-dizzy psyches can muster,
I understand the pain that these lies
cause myself and others
is as evil as sunrise, as sinister as sunset.*

Finish by sitting quietly, praying that the fruits of your practice might inspire all beings to be released.

# USING THE WHEELS to cultivate compassion and insight into another ego

### 1. Set your intention
Begin by thinking of those you come into contact with every day, and the impact you have on them when you receive them with compassion versus when you receive them with reactivity. Set an intention to enter this practice deeply not just for yourself, but for them.

### 2. Circle
Begin by circling once around all 12 wheels, keeping in mind a person you are having trouble with. Make a list of the wheels this person seems, in your eyes, to struggle with. Choose the wheel that best describes the qualities you find most challenging in this person.

### 3. Feel their inner life
Read the text corresponding to this wheel's window of sanity, then feel your way around this wheel, each time pausing at the window to feel into what this person's inner life and outer circumstances must be like as a result of their continually passing over this window and descending into egoic automation, if not full-scale crisis.

### 4. Inquire
Ask: What is my gut response when they descend into each of the unconscious phases of this wheel? Is this a way of joining them in their spin? What if their soul came into my life to help me wake up as as the compassionate, witnessing center of this wheel? Could they be my divinely ordained teacher and liberator?

### 5. Be released

Continue feeling your way around this wheel until your heart softens, not just for the suffering this person has endured, but for the ways you have suffered by reacting to their spinning circumference. (This may take numerous sittings.)

### 6. Return to your first impression list

When your work with this wheel feels complete, return to your first impression list and ask yourself, *Which wheel is crying out loudest for a witness now?* Repeat the practice with that wheel.

### 7. Dedication: Forgive the dream

When you are finished, dedicate your practice to the countless number of souls who are, even now, being ravaged by these wheels:

> *Now that I see how gradations of lying*
> *are the best our staggering, wheel-dizzy psyches can muster,*
> *I understand the pain that these lies*
> *cause myself and others*
> *is as evil as sunrise, as sinister as sunset.*

Finish by sitting quietly, praying that the fruits of your practice might inspire all beings to be released.

# If you enjoyed
## this book *and would like to dive deeper into the Astrodharmic worldview, you can learn many other techniques for using astrology as a path of awakening by enrolling in the three-month, online Styles of Awakening Training. More than just a course in archetypal literacy, this is a unique and comprehensive Astrodharmic mind training designed to help you crack the code of personality and live in more steady contact with people's souls. For course description, testimonials and training dates, visit astrodharma.com.*

*You may also wish to sign up for the free, monthly Styles of Awakening Newsletter. Pithy, playful and cutting-edge, this one-of-a-kind newsletter is chock full of articles, transit updates, poetry, video meditations, "sacred soundbites" and special subscriber discounts, all designed with one goal in mind: to keep you mad enough to be mortal—sane enough to disappear.*

## "Hunter Reynolds is one of the most interesting astrological thinkers out there."

—*Rob Brezsny*
  *Free Will Astrology columnist*
  *& author of* Pronoia: The Antidote to Paranoia

You who takes equal delight in firing the synapses
of inspiring saints and vitriolic talk show hosts:
Make us a pitiful judge of character,
seeing only your infinitely colorful and amusing
styles of awakening.

# About the Author

HUNTER REYNOLDS is an astrological counselor, teacher, writer and dharma poet. Born in Chicago and raised in an intentional community based on the teachings of 17th century mystic Emmanuel Swedenborg, he has since been deeply influenced by Advaita and Buddhist thought. A full-time astrologer since 2002, Hunter weaves the meditative insights of the east with the psychological insights of western astrology, creating a unique form of counseling called "Astrodharma" in which the astrological archetypes are understood as styles of awakening.

In addition to offering professional phone and in-person consultations worldwide, he has a passion for teaching students how to practice astrology as a path of awakening via his intensive, three-month archetypal literacy course entitled "The Styles of Awakening Training." Courses and resources for continuing students are currently under development.

He is the author of *Brave New Prayers,* a book of edgy, non-dual prayers. His website is www.astrodharma.org.

Some seeds only germinate in a forest fire.
There are flowers in us that have been waiting
for exactly these conditions.

# About Flamingseed Press

FLAMINGSEED PRESS is a boundary-crossing experiment in publishing. The mission: to publish soulful books that grapple with the challenge of marrying spirit to earth. They cross boundaries of culture and religion, generation and place, genre and paradigm, all with the intention of taking fast-changing times and challenging circumstances as inspiration to find more wise and soulful ways to live on our endangered planet, cultivating connection rather than division, love rather than fear.

This book is the first in a series from emerging voices on innovative practices to help restore the link in each of us between spirit and earth. The series will include books on meditation, art as spiritual practice, writing as spiritual practice, the blending of astrology and dharma, soulful poetry, and practical mysticism. Sign up for the newsletter at flamingseed.com for occasional bits of inspiration from flamingseed publisher Jane Brunette, and to be notified when new titles are released.

**flamingseedpress.com**

# Mystic poetry
# from Flamingseed Press

### Brave New Prayers
### by Hunter Reynolds

Imagine Rumi raised on YouTube—
not to mention corporate greed and all
the trappings of racy Western culture.
What brave new metaphors might he
call upon to convey his astounding
lucid confusion?

*bravenewprayers.com*

### Grasshopper Guru
### by Jane Brunette

These poems were born from a
long cycle of retreat outside of the
consumer matrix where wisdom
and quiet heartbreak emerged
from fading dreams and dilemmas
while darkness, sky and the small
details of the natural world served
as guru and monastery.

*flamingseed.com*

**flamingseedpress.com**